I0789715

Write the Book Right Now

Quick Guide to Writing Your Story

By: Cynthia Young

"There is no greater agony than bearing an untold story inside you." — Maya Angelou

Write the Book Right Now: Quick Guide to Writing Your Story

Copyright © 2020 by Cynthia Young

All rights reserved. No part of this publication may be reproduced, distributed, or transmitted in any form or by any means, including photocopying, recording, or other electronic or mechanical methods, without the prior written permission of the publisher, except in the case of brief quotations embodied in critical reviews and certain other noncommercial uses permitted by copyright law.

Visit the author's website www.allthingscynthiayoung.com

Contents

Introduction

Part 1: Preparing to Write

Part 2: Writing

Part 3: Editing & Proofreading

Part 4: Self-Publishing

Bonus

Write the Book Right Now

Quick Guide to Writing Your Story

Have you been wanting to write a book? Do you have this burning desire to share your story? Do you have a unique story to tell that the world needs to hear?

But there's one problem: you have no clue where to begin. You don't know how to put your words on paper. You've never written a book before. Well, I have great news for you! What if I told you that you can indeed craft your story and get it into the hands of readers who will be better persons because of you sharing your story.

Writing our stories and sharing them is one of the most powerful ways to grow and make that journey from the head to the heart. You are the only person who can tell your story, and it is only by writing, sharing and releasing it that you can begin to rewrite your future.

This quick guide will teach you the process to completing your manuscript. Whether you want to publish your story or write it to keep for yourself, this guide will help you learn the most effective ways to convey your life experiences onto the page.

I love to read memoirs and biographies in fact 70 percent of the books I read these days are of others sharing their story. I was eventually inspired to share my story in writing when I published my first book in 2012. After receiving questions from so many people about how to write a book, I said I must share with you how I did it. Writing and helping others to pursue purpose are two of my most favorite things to do.

Writing a book is a great way to get your message out to the world. My prayer is that you will find this guide helpful in guiding you to crafting your story. I know all too well what it feels like to have a story to tell and not know where to begin writing. It doesn't have to take years to write your book but how long it takes depends on you.

Now, Get Ready Let's Go!!

Yours Truly,

Cynthia

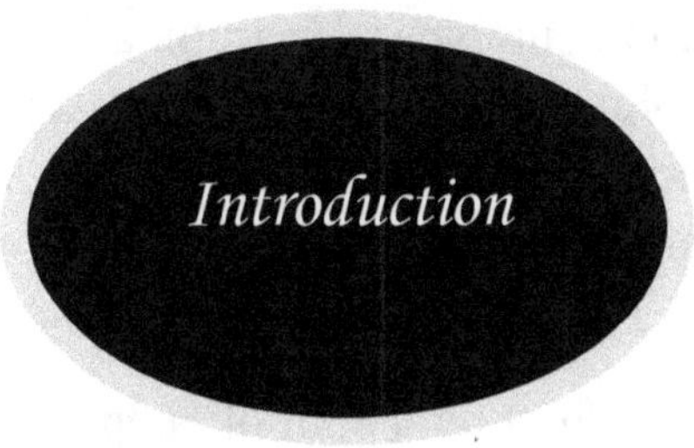

Others Need To Hear Your Story

If no one has ever told you, I want to be the first to tell you that you have a story in fact everyone has a story, and no one can tell your story quite like you can. You must embrace your story at all costs because guess what, it's your story and your truth. Can't nobody in this world take away or add to your story. It's yours! All of it! The good, the bad, the pretty and the ugly!

When I first decided to share my story in my first book in 2012 "From da Club 2 da Church House", I didn't know how others would receive what I put on the inside of those pages of my book. If I can be totally honest with you, I was uneasy about how what I shared would affect me and what others perceived of me.

I shared some truths in my book that nobody but me and God had known about. Well maybe a few other people may have known some of what I shared but for the most part, a lot of what I shared was my first time sharing with anyone. My family and friends were even surprised and had no idea some of things I had been through.

When you begin to embrace your truth, all of it and not just bits and pieces of it, you begin discovering a part of you that usually stays hidden for most people. Not everyone is ready to embrace their story and their truth let alone share with others.

Guilt, shame and regret hold a lot of people back from fully embracing their truth. I used to feel ashamed as the years went by as I looked back over my life. My teenage years were full of experiences that a young girl my age should have never been exposed to. Sex and bad habits became a part of my world before I even entered my teenage years. It was before I entered high school that I began heading down a path of destruction with no clear roadmap on where I would eventually end up.

When I became pregnant at the age of 16 and dropped out of high school a year later, I just knew my life was over from that point forward. I share all this to say that we all have a past and a story. Some of us are not proud of where we been in life, but it's our experiences and it has helped to shape us into the persons we are today.

Let's look at it this way; what if I told you everything you been through wasn't for you but for someone else. What you had to endure and overcome all happened so you can be the one to share with others how you survived and made it out. Not everyone will share their story especially if it involves feelings of guilt and shame.

We get so wrapped up in what others will say and think as if others haven't been through the same thing or even worse. We can't allow other folks opinions of us stop us from doing what we believe we need to be doing.

With that said, I hope you would have a better understanding of how extremely imperative it is that you share your story. There are people who lives depend on you and your willingness to share. And don't worry, you don't have to tell every intimate detail you've ever experienced but you should make it a point to share what really matters.

You have a gift and your personal story will help get people to their next best step and it involves you stepping up. You don't need be an expert to write your personal story. I sure wasn't an expert when I started out on my journey of writing. I just wanted to write and get my story our there because I knew there were people who needed to hear it. I've always journaled my thoughts and what was going on around me.

Read To Write

One of the most common pieces of advice for writers is to read. Reading is equally about exiting and entering, about going away and going nowhere. Reading early in the morning is like having one more dream, like lying down just a little longer in the strange, sweet gauze of sleep.

You don't have to be a professional writer to write your story however I do believe when you read other's stories through memoirs and autobiographies, it helps to ease your flow of writing. I have learned this as I have read and as I have reviewed my own work and the work of others.

The craft of writing is to describe something so that someone else can see it. What do you expect of others as you read, and what do you expect of yourself as a writer?

Write for the right reasons. Write real. Write with the understanding, that some lives or secrets do not belong to us.

Write knowing that there are those who will inevitably walk away.

You might feel better after your story is written but after it is read, after the critics have had their say, after you have overheard your neighbors at the block party whispering, after your sister has rebuked your way of remembering, how will you feel? Be prepared. Be cognizant. Move forward, but with caution.

Start small by making notes to yourself. Go out and buy yourself a blank-page journal or jot down notes in your phone's notetaking app. Launch a blog. Write about what is happening right now so that you can learn to write well about what happened yesterday.

Journal keeping, diary making, blogging—it's all a curious thing, but it isn't a book But it's a start, an inroad, a gesture. It tells us something about ourselves, records the details of our living, puts dialogue somewhere safe so that we can retrieve it later, talks back to us about us.

A journal is written so that a journal might be studied. A journal is where the work-in-progress writer begins to wrestle his- or herself down, begins to understand or tussle with his or her own authority and authenticity. Teach yourself the range of your own voice.

You Are Qualified

Your life experiences qualify you to write

- You don't need to be a certified expert to write a book
- You don't need to be an expert writer to write a book

- You don't need to write a specific number of pages
- It doesn't have to take years to write a book
- You do not have to be a bestseller to become an author

God Will Bless the Work

of Your Hands…

Focus on Being Of Service

Through Your Writing

and Making A Difference…

D id you prepare before you sat down to write? Have a plan before you sit down to write. You must be able to answer the following questions.

- What do I have to say and why should anyone care?
- What do I want to write about?
- What are the key objectives I want to teach those who read my book?
- What problems am I helping people to solve?
- Who is my target audience?
- When do I want to have the book written?

Research

Research is the bread and butter of your creations because your work is based in fact. Research is any form of inquiry that helps you increase your understanding of what happened. Research may include digging up old photos, reading newspapers and histories of the time you're writing about, or studying memoirs by authors who have undergone similar challenges.

If your book is about illness, abuse, or other social and psychological themes, research may mean reading studies or talking to professionals on the subject. It may involve traveling to the places where events occurred. In fact, going back to places in your past can be incredibly powerful, and provide the emotional, sensory, and concrete details necessary to give life to your scenes.

Interviewing is another powerful form of research; what do others remember about that time and the people involved? And don't forget the library. The library offers a rich resource of materials not to be found online, as well as staff to help you find what you're looking for.

Research is important for fact checking your memories, giving your book a high level of credibility. Research is also important to help you understand and interpret the scenes you write while placing your story in the larger context of life. It helps you discover and uncover your universally important message.

Keep A Daily Journal
Your journal is where you work out your ideas or write when you don't have anything formal to write about. Set aside 15 minutes every day to write in your journal to stay disciplined or get in the writing spirit before you start working on your book.

Writing in a journal isn't about getting perfect writing. Journal writing is about practicing writing and exploring your ideas. It should be something that won't be judged, graded, or read by others. It's most effective if it's in a safe place for you to experiment.

Your journal is primarily for writing, but there's no rule that says you couldn't also paste in pictures or draw illustrations. By recording those thoughts, you're creating a powerful tool to discover your hopes, dreams, and fears.

Set Up Microsoft Word Document

Open a new document in Microsoft Word and save it as (Book Title) Manuscript. For a 6"x9" book, start by changing the paper size and the margins to match the dimensions of a 6" x 9" book (these instructions are applicable to whatever book trim size you choose).

Start by double-clicking on the ruler at the top of your document and bring up the document formatting window. Click on the "Margins" tab, then the "Page Setup" button. Click on "Paper Size," then "Manage Custom Sizes."

Make your header and footer 0.5" or 0.44" to match the top and bottom print margins. Check "mirror margins" to set your book up like a printed book spread.

Set your size to the standard **12-point font** and font to: **Times New Roman**. You also might want to decrease or increase the space between your lines. You can set it "single" if you want it to be tight or "double" if you like a lot of space in-between. I recommend 1.5 for a happy medium.

Chapters

Next, click the "Layout" tab. If you would like your chapters to all start on a right-hand page, set each chapter as a new section break, and set those new sections to start on an odd page.

For headers and footers, select the "different odd and even" option if you want to have an author name on one side and the title of the book or chapter name on the other side. Select "different first page" if you don't want to have your headers at the beginning of each chapter.

Now click "OK" to apply the changes to the whole document. The page size is now set to 6″ x 9″ as opposed to the 8.5″ by 11″ you probably started out with.

Basic Formatting

Let's continue with some basic formatting. Turn on "show all non-printing characters" to help you identify what type of breaks you are using.

Assuming you have the text of your book and your chapters defined, you will want to include a title page and a copyright page for the year of publication.

Do not hit the enter button several times to create a new page. Instead, go to "Insert > Break > Page Break" to define a break in the page.

Now, you can design a **Title Page**. Type in your book title and increase the font size. Bring it down to about the middle of your first page. On this page you simply type the book title, subtitle and your name. Look at a book in your personal library. Where their title is listed on a full page is called a Title Page. Follow the format of your choice.

Now, add your copyright information to be on the backside of that title page. That will be on page two, so insert another page break.

Include the publication year and anything else you would like to list. **Copyright Information** is typically down at the bottom of the page.

What Is Copyright?

Copyright refers to the legal right of the owner of intellectual property. In simpler terms, copyright is the right to copy. This means that the original creators of products and anyone they give authorization to are the only ones with the exclusive right to reproduce the work.

Identify if you will include a **Foreword Page** & If So, Who will write it. On the next page in your Word document type the word: **Foreword** (notice the correct spelling) and think about who you would like to write it. Usually someone who knows you and can endorse your book as it relates to the content shared. This could be your coach or mentor, close friend or a respected person in your industry; etc.

On the **Dedication Page**, you will type the word Dedication at the top and type out who you would like to dedicate your book to (usually one person or a group of people.)

On **Acknowledgments Page** of your book type the word Acknowledgements at the top and begin to write out who you would like to give praise to. These are people who supported you and helped make this project happen or added value to your life along the way.

Include **About the Author Page** (Bio) at the top of the page and insert your bio. Make sure your bio is relevant to who you are and what you do. View sample About the Author pages from books within your personal library if you need an example. A professional photo can be inserted to add to this page.

Table of Contents and More

Insert a "section break." Then, go to the "Insert" dropdown, select "Table of Contents," pick a style, and insert it. Now you'll see a "Table of Contents" list with page numbers.

Next, to set your footers, double-click in the area below your text. You'll see they're defined as odd and even page footers. Go to "Insert Page Numbers." Choose to have them all align to the "Outside" or "Centered." If you have them all aligned to the same side, half of them are will face the gutter and inside of your book. If you have them on the "Inside," they are ALL going to be on your gutter side.

You can choose whether to "Show numbers on the first page" by clicking or unclicking the appropriate box.

Next, double-click above your text to insert a header. If you chose earlier to set it up as different odd and even headers, you can put the "Author Name" on one side and the title of the book on the other.

Next is your text alignment, left-align, center-align, right-align, and justified. A lot of books are designed with justified text but select what fits best for your book. Review other books in which you like their format to provide you with a sample.

The **Introduction Page** can include a short story, facts that lead to the content you will be sharing within the pages of your book or can provide a guide on how the reader can get the most out of your resource.

You want to spend some time here as well to ensure the content is interesting enough for your reader and adds value. This is another determining factor as it relates to someone purchasing your book.

Next, insert a "Section break" (we recommend the "next odd page"), then highlight the chapter text. Click on the formatting style in the formatting palette or at the top of your document and select "Heading." Now this will be defined as a "Chapter Heading."

Go ahead and find where you designated chapter 2 and repeat the same instructions as before: insert a "section break odd page" and mark the chapter text as a "Heading."

Create An Outline

Your outline to your book is what a business plan is to your business. It serves as a blueprint when writing your book & will prevent writer's block if you take the time to complete the steps below.

Here is where you will open a new Word document and this time title it "(Book Title) Outline". Following the format insert chapter titles for each, key objective or goal for each section while keeping the reader in mind. If you are sharing a portion of your story or any content, clearly identify why you are sharing it. This will help keep your motives clear and ensure you are adding value to the reader.

This portion may take quite a few hours or even a few days to complete. Remember, your outline serves as a blueprint for your book. When you prepare to write your book, you will print out your outline and use it as a guide while you are on your computer typing content for each chapter.

Your outline can also be sent to whoever you desire to write your foreword so they have a clear idea of what you are writing about and the value you will bring to your reader. Most people do not read full manuscripts anymore when deciding to endorse someone's book.

Remember to copy and paste the outline below into a Word document and it's okay if you have more than 5 chapters.

Book Outline:

I. Chapter 1: (Insert Title) Objective/Goal: (My key objective for chapter 1 is….) Here I am sharing…. (Use full and complete thoughts & include any quotes or research and insert them here.)

a.

b.

c.

II. Chapter 2: (Insert Title) Objective/Goal: (My key objective for chapter 2 is….) Here I am sharing…. (Use full and complete thoughts & include any quotes or research and insert them here.)

a.

b.

c.

III. Chapter 3: (Insert Title) Objective/Goal: (My key objective for chapter 3 is….) Here I am sharing…. (Use full and complete thoughts & include any quotes or research and insert them here.)

a.

b.

c.

IV. Chapter 4: (Insert Title) Objective/Goal: (My key objective for chapter 4 is….) Here I am sharing…. (Use full and complete thoughts & include any quotes or research and insert them here.)

a.

b.

c.

V. Chapter 5: (Insert Title) Objective/Goal: (My key objective for chapter 5 is….) Here I am sharing…. (Use full and complete thoughts & include any quotes or research and insert them here.)

a.

b.

c.

Feel free to insert more roman numerals if you have more than 5 chapters, simply copy and paste and update chapter number. This is just a sample to get you going.

After you have completed your outline, save it, and then open your manuscript file and change the font size to 16 and insert chapter titles on each page.

For example. On page 9 (after the introduction) insert a page break and type out the following:

Chapter 1

(Chapter Title)

Next, insert another page break and type Chapter 2 (Chapter Title). Feel free to use books in your personal library as a guide.

You should now have created two Word Documents: Your Manuscript File and Your Outline.

Create A Writing Schedule

Every writer has a vision of being able to sit down and write a complete prize-winning chapter in one sitting, but this isn't realistic. To get a flow going on a regular basis you will need to implement a writing routine.

Forming a regular writing habit builds stakes, holds you accountable to your goals, and keeps you on track as a result.

Building a solid, consistent routine will help you write, and write well, even when you're not feeling motivated or inspired.

A writing routine will be different for everyone in terms of your environment, time availability, aims, goals — the lot. Even so, if you follow these tips for establishing and, more importantly, sticking to a routine, you can't go far wrong.

1. Schedule your writing time

Try to choose a time and a place so that other things can work around your writing time, not vice versa. This way, you'll be able to get into the habit of writing — even when you don't feel like it.

If you wait for this time to come around naturally, especially in increasingly hectic lives, the hours required to achieve our goals of writing are not going to clock in.

This time should be non-negotiable. Even if you can't write every day, make sure you have time locked in multiple times a week.

Nothing is stopping you from starting right now: literally, open your phone and schedule writing time into your calendar — this will make you stick to it. Put in a realistic amount of time that you know you can afford, make sure it's more than once a week, highlight it in something bright that you can't ignore, and set an alarm to remind you.

2. Make this writing time sacred

Whether it's every workday evening from 8 to 10, or three mornings a week starting at 7, don't let anything get in the way of your writing. You've scheduled this time into your life, and it must be granted importance.

This also means that writing time is for writing and writing only. Being lax with it will hold back your progress. If you set aside two hours to write, and in that time answer your emails, do a laundry load, and check Facebook, you'll probably end up doing half an hour of writing, maximum. That would move the needle extremely slowly.

Research and planning should be done outside these hours. Writing time is just that: time to put pen to paper or fingers to keyboard.

3. Quantify your progress

To know the progress you're making, set yourself a word count goal per day or per week. The power of setting tiny, achievable goals cannot be overstated.

We as humans love having these little wins. Hitting daily goals gives us little boosts and makes us feel good about what we're doing. Writing can be frustrating, so word count goals give you control over at least one of the factors of the writing process.

The fun side of this is rewarding yourself. Crossing things off that calendar, physically printing off pages you've written and adding them to a done pile — anything that gives you a sense of public, visible achievement is worth it. As a writer, you have to reward yourself when you reach your goals, which is much easier when these goals are concrete and achievable.

4. Publicize it

Your public could just be your friends and loved ones so share with them you're writing a book. This puts pressure on you, as does publicizing your goals.

If you have something visible, like a calendar that shows your self-set deadlines or workloads, this can help keep you accountable to goals that would otherwise be easy to pretend you never made.

Starting a blog and publicizing your progress is another way to give you that extra incentive, as you don't want to look bad in front of your followers by not meeting your goals.

Pro Tip

Be intentional about making time because

there is no perfect time to write.

Know what environment you work best in and use this to your advantage. Whether it's the bustle of a coffee shop or a silent room at home, you know where and when you produce your best work.

Appreciate that these are all estimates, especially if you don't have a contract yet. A writing routine will give you direction, even if you don't have an actual deadline. It will help orient you, rather than just writing whenever you feel like it.

Writing is a challenge, but so rewarding. The key is to stick to it. Establishing and dedicating yourself to the process says that you believe in yourself, and that you can do it.

Handling Writer's Block

Writer's block is a condition in which a writer is unable to think of what should be written next. If you experience writer's block, you may be unable to develop a new piece of content or finish an existing piece. You may feel as if your thinking has become clouded, drained of inspiration, and frustration has set in.

It's like going through a maze and realizing you've made the wrong turn, only to end up at a dead end; you've hit a mental "block." Anyone can end up with writer's block.

The condition could be caused by several different things. Some believe that an author may lack creativity or knowledge surrounding a particular topic – and this may contribute to the block. In other cases, a writer may have no emotional inspiration in regard to the topic they are writing about. Running out of inspiration makes it very difficult to focus.

Other causes for the condition include; environmental changes, mental illness, relationship troubles, increased stress, or perfectionism. Oftentimes authors experience writer's block when they are pressured into writing a piece of content with a specific deadline. Feeling a sense of intimidation, being unable to work at your own pace, or constantly trying to out-do yourself may also contribute to the block.

You can overcome writer's block by first determining the cause of your writer's block. Was it caused by a lack of inspiration or material? It is important to realize that a solution for writer's block in one person may not be beneficial for another individual.

Coping strategies: It is important to understand some coping strategies that you can use when you hit a block while writing. Most people are unaware of what they should do during the onset of the block.

- **Avoid perfectionism**: If you have writer's block, your initial rough draft may suck – which is fine because it's a draft. The goal is to get something written even if it is complete trash in terms of your standards. Many writers over-think and over-analyze what they write, critiquing everything along the way. Stop nit-picking every detail and just write… even if it's bad, you can always edit it later.

- **Brainstorming:** If you have hit a block, one way to get around it is to brainstorm. Think of ideas for your writing and write them all down. Even if you think they are "bad" ideas, just write them down anyway. The idea behind brainstorming is to change your perception and let the creative juices flow.

- **Change environment:** Your environment can have a big influence on how easy or difficult it is to write. If you are attempting to write in a noisy environment with people talking, music playing, or the hustle and bustle of the outside world – this could be interfering with your concentration. Anything in your environment that is detrimental to your concentration has potential to cause writer's block.

- **Cut distractions:** A lot of people, especially students work on writing with their headphones playing music, their social media accounts open (i.e. Facebook), and their cell phone alerts turned on. These distractions not only make the process of writing less efficient, but they can cause us to lose the flow of our work. If you get a good start on your writing, but suddenly get caught up texting your friend, you may now have writer's block. Cut back on all distractions and focus on the topic at hand.

- **Find inspiration**: If you are lacking inspiration, do your best to find a little bit. This may mean reading some inspirational quotes, reading new material, or thinking about people that inspire you. It may be something as simple as having a conversation with a friend that gives you your next idea.

- **Read something**: Reading primes your brain with new ideas and perspectives on various topics. If you are caught up in a mental "block" take the time to just read something, even if it's completely random. Chances are good that when you're done reading, you'll be able to think of something to write.

- **Research:** Perhaps you have writer's block because you aren't very familiar with the topic you're writing about. You can't expect to pull material out of your brain that was never there in the first place. Take the time to do a bit of research and take some notes – this will give you a better understanding of the topic and some general ideas.

- **Relaxation**: If you are stressed, one of the best ways to overcome writer's block is to relax.

- **Sleep:** You may be experiencing writer's block because you haven't gotten enough sleep. When we lose sleep, it becomes difficult to think clear about anything, let alone write.

- **Take a break:** If you are staring at your document and are racking your brain for ideas or what to say next, sometimes the best thing you can do is take a break. Give yourself a break to psychologically "refresh" and then come back to your writing mentally recharged.

If you have writer's block, you are not alone – many people share your frustration. Over time, you will find solutions and coping strategies that help you get past writer's block.

Pro Tip

Stay Committed

Persevere through Writers Block

Copy edit & Proofreading

Copy editing is the stage in which a piece of writing, the "copy," is reviewed and edited to improve its readability. You can copy edit your manuscript yourself or you can hire someone to complete this process of completing your book for you. As a copy editor, you'll look for technical issues within a piece of writing:

- **Format errors.** The number one priority for a copy editor is to highlight and suggest corrections to grammatical errors, spelling errors, and punctuation errors. Although these areas may be tackled by a separate proofreader, a copy editor still needs to address them as they see them, as they may affect the content of the work itself.

- **Enforces flow**. Too many words can bog down a text and confuse the reader. A good copy editor will be able to eliminate superfluous sentences and tighten phrasing in order to help streamline the writer's story or message.

- **Checks for consistency**. The copy editor job requires you to be detail oriented. One of the main responsibilities of a copy editor is to comb through a given work and check to make sure details are kept consistent, such as descriptions of settings and characters. If a house is white in one chapter, then suddenly brown in the next, it is the copy editor's job to notice and change that detail.

- **Fact checks.** The copy editing process can also involve research, especially when editing nonfiction works. If there is no specialized fact checker working on a publication, the copy editor may need to verify dates and events to maintain factual accuracy.
- **Do a final read.** Be sure to check your own work. It is important that your editing services have improved the readability of the writing, not complicated it. Although there will most likely be a proofing stage, try to ensure the text is as error-free as possible.

Pro Tip

Proofread your book backward. It may sound silly, but your brain concentrates on the story when you read, so proofread out of order. Perhaps last chapter first.

Self-Publish a Book on Amazon

Step 1. Create an Amazon Kindle Direct Publishing (KDP) Account. If you already have an Amazon account, use it to sign into the KDP system. If not, create a new KDP account. Because it's your first time signing in with KDP, you'll need to accept the terms of use. Once you do that, you'll see your Amazon Author dashboard. Follow instructions to continue setting up account.

Step 2. Upload your manuscript. (word doc or pdf)

Step 3. Upload your book cover. People do judge books by their covers. Like it or not, this is 100% true, and there's a ton of marketing research to back it up. If you want your book to sell, the cover design has to be professional.

Do not design your own book cover. Even something as simple as the cover font can ruin your cover if you don't know what you're doing. If you want to be taken seriously as a published Author, hire a professional cover designer (and listen to them.)

Step 4. Preview your book. Once you've uploaded your manuscript and cover, you can preview your book using the

Kindle Previewer. Do not rush through your preview. Read and test everything.

Step 5. ISBN and Publisher.

Step 6. Choose your royalty and pricing. Choose between 35% and 70% for your royalty. For most Authors, the 70% royalty will pay more. That seems obvious, but it does add some pricing limitations as well as a slightly different royalty calculation.

Choose Amazon.com as your primary marketplace, then set the list price. The price in other marketplaces will be set according to exchange rates, but you can set each one manually if you want to.

Step 7. Save to draft until you're ready. Choose "Save as Draft" until you're ready to choose a publishing date and launch your book. Think through every aspect of your book's marketing before you publish. That goes beyond your book's cover, layout, pricing, and marketing plan.

BONUS: 10 Ways to Market Your Book

- Share on Social Media
- Make a book trailer
- Contact local library about getting your book in the library
- Send an email to your list. Give them a reason to buy your book
- Create a series of YouTube videos where the author sits reading small sections of the book
- Host a Book Signing
- Contact local Newspaper
- Contact local bookstores (Barnes & Noble)
- Participate in vendor events
- Share Facebook live or podcast

www.ingramcontent.com/pod-product-compliance
Lightning Source LLC
Chambersburg PA
CBHW070747240726
48654CB00010B/1191